Table of Contents

SECRETS

OF

LORD SHANI

By

GURU GAURAV ARYA

(Astrologer & Researcher)

Language: English, Character set, encoding: UTF-8, Graphics by – Author, Formating by – Author, Cover Page Design by- Author

About The Book

Lord Shani Dev has been known for his unequaled significance in Hindu Mythology and Astrology. Lord Shani Dev is called the God of Justice, and for those who need justice, it is very fruitful to go under the protection of Shani Dev. Through this book, I would like to share my knowledge and research done so far about the secrets of Shani Dev, which we all need to know. And by understanding those secrets, we can appreciate Shani dev better. Through this book, I have tried to light the unspoken mysteries, facts like why the Lord is called Shani? About Shani Dev's color, why is the Lord considered the god of justice?

Generally, every one of us has come across lord Shani dev somewhere; many people have a lot of misconceptions about Lord Shani. Moreover, astrologers known for making lives simpler are themselves spreading fear towards Lord Shani among people in the names of Sadhe Sati, Bad position of Shani dev in Birth Chart, etc. Mainly people consider lord Shani dev as the god of punishment. I have concluded that Lord Shani dev is the God of Justice and the punisher and destroyer of injustice. We should keep in mind that whenever Shani Dev punishes someone, he does so only to complete the account of his deeds. I will reveal the unique kinds of secrets through this book so that the seekers and all humans understand their deeds and be ready for the fruit that comes from them and any fallacy. On average, every person worships Shani Dev and gets his blessings in today's world. However, it is to be noted that whenever someone worships any Shakti or Devi or deity or has reverence towards them, then at the same time, that person should have complete knowledge about the same power. As we all have come across this statement that, "Little knowledge is dangerous," therefore it is essential to have complete information or at least some basic information so that you can get maximum results. The secrets of Shani Dev described in this book are somehow related to his personality and karma. The seeker and a layperson can easily understand and worship accordingly. Also, when a seeker understands and knows about their secrets, he will become closer to Shani dev. Some of the unique mysteries relate to his name Shani are like what is the meaning of Shani?

- Why is his color black?
- Why is his symbol black?
- Why is Mustard oil offered to Shani Dev?
- Why is Shani Dev the God of Kalyuga?

And many more, I will discuss all these topics in detail.

About The Author

Guru Gaurav Arya is an Indian Astrologer and Researcher. He has been practicing astrology since 2007. After completing many complicated astrological cases, Guru is providing astrological services globally. By passion, he is an Astrologer/Paranormal Expert and Occult master. He was a Mechanical Engineer; however, after completing Engineering Projects, he started Astrology Consulting. Now, Guru Gaurav Arya is a leading name in Astrology. He has written many books in Hindi languages like "Shree Shani Samhita" "Yantra Tatvam."

Achievements

In 2017, Guru Gaurav Arya was awarded Jyotish Shree by the CM of Uttarakhand, and in 2018 he was awarded by Jyotish Vibhushan by CM of Uttarakhand. Also, in 2019, he was awarded the award for excellence in astrology.

He is a world-known Vedic astrologer with expertise in all the Vedic astrology/Modern Occult Science/Paranormal Expertise departments. Working for the best of his Pupils, Gaurav Arya has been practicing a range of services in Vedic and Occult Science/Paranormal Expertise over the past 15 years. He has a supernatural vision to solve problems with ancient and modern capabilities. Whether small or big, every issue has ended after meeting the eminent name in Astrology. Analyzing every situation deeply, he has the perfect resolution for everyone with the assistance of occult and simple astrological remedies.

Guru Gaurav Arya

Indian Astrologer & Researcher

Jyotish Shree, Jyotish Vibhushan, Paranormal Expert

Indian Mythologist, Spiritual Author.

Follow on Twitter @Gurugauravarya

This book is dedicated to

MY Guru

TRIKAL DARSHI Shri SHANI DEV

Introduction Of Lord Shani Dev

Though Lord Shani Dev does not need any introduction, he is the epitome of justice for all sinners. I am speechless here to describe the glory of my Lord Shani dev in words, and it is only the unshakable faith in the Lord that I am trying to educate people about the delight I gained by worshipping him.

- Father of Lord Shani- **Surya Narayan.**
- Mother of Lord Shani- **Chadevi, Suvarna.**
- Shani Dev's brother- **Yamraj.**
- Shani Dev sister- **Yamuna Devi.**
- Shani Dev Guru- **Lord Shiva Shankar.**
- Birth Place- **Saurashtra, Gujarat.**
- Shani Dev Gotra- **Kashyap.**
- Complexion – **Dark Black.**
- Nature- **Tyagi, ascetic, vision, grumpy, profound, lucid.**
- Friends- **Balaji, Hanumanji, Bhairav.**
- Other Names- **Chhayasut, Suryaputra, Konastha, Pingalo, Babhru, Raudratak, Sauri, Shanaichar, Krishnamand, Krishna.**
- Planet Friends- **Guru, Venus, Rahu, Mercury.**
- Zodiac Friends- **Taurus, Gemini, Virgo, Libra.**
- Own Zodiac- **Capricorn, Aquarius.**
- Ownconstellation- **Pushya, Anuradha, Uttara-Bhadrapada.**
- Area of Saturn- **Petroleum, iron, steel, industry, press, etc.**
- Expertise- **Justice, Tantra, Punishment.**
- Incarnation- **Lord Vishnu.**
- Istha Devta- **Lord Krishna.**
- By Nature- **Cruel and Kind**

Why is Lord Shani Dev called Shani?

WHY IS LORD SHANI DEV is called 'Shani'?

The word Shani has been derived from Sanskrit "Shani Kamith Sha' which means slow. Hence, we can say that Shani means very slow. Even in actual practice, Saturn is also very slow in its movement, which represents "Shani Dev." In Vedic Astrology, Saturn is considered the planet of God Shani Dev. Saturn performs a vital role in the horoscope. Without Lord Shani, every horoscope is incomplete; also, the transit of Saturn performs a crucial role in predicting the future. Now, I will discuss why Shani Dev is called Shani? In the lines described above, the meaning of Shani", i.e., very slow.

Since childhood, the Lord was very aggressive and naughty. Because Shani is the son of Sun and Chhaya and the Sun's power is aggressive, and the power of Chahhya is not aggressive, resultantly Shani dev is more aggressive by nature. The childhood of Shani Dev was not that good, and his childhood was never trouble-free just because he was very naughty and always tried to fight with everyone. Shani has another meaning which means brighter. The Sun continuously brightens the universe, being his son (Lord Shani) also shines with his light. But this does not happen by combining the Sun & Chhaya. Chhaya was scorched, the opposite result of which can see inside Lord Shani. The second reason to call Lord Shani is Saturn; Saturn is the Representative of God Shani Dev. And Saturn is also a very slow-moving planet. Saturn moved from one zodiac sign to another in Vedic astrology in 2.5 years. And the Dasha of Shani is 19 years, and Sade Sati of Shani is 7.5 years, so we can understand how slow Saturn is? Now, I want to tell you the meaning of Shani dev for 108 other names. We have read the reason for his name as Shani in the above lines.

However, Shani also has the following names, which signify the qualities of Lord Shani Dev as under.

❖ - Sanaischara

The One Who Moves slowly because Shani means slow and Chara means movement. So we can say Sanaischara

❖ - Shanta

The Peaceful One in Sanskrit Shanta means fulfillment of Silence.

❖ - Sarvabhishta-pradayin

The Fulfiller of All Desires means God Shani can fill all desires of native.

❖ - Sharanya

The Protector, Shani dev, is also known as a god protector who can cover you in the opposite situation.

❖ - Varenya

The Most Excellent One, Who is the skilled one in technology.

❖ Sarvesha

The Lord of All, Who is doing everything in the universe to make balance,

❖ - Saumya

The Mild One. God of mercy and ready to forgive everyone.

❖ - Suravandhaya

The One Who is Fit to be Worshipped by Suras. It is a fact God Shani have good skill in Music and Sur, Musical instruments, Raag, etc.

❖ Suralokaviharin

The One Who Wanders in the World of Suras, Shani dev always wanders in suur Lok to enhance the skill of sura's.

❖ - Sukhasanopavishta

The One Seated Upon a Comfortable. As I know that God Shani always sat upon a black Singhsan.

❖ - Sundara

The Beautiful One. As I know, Shani dev is black, but features and muhut and hairs are so good, so Shani dev is Sundra.

❖ - Ghana

The Solid One. Ghana is made of iron, so Shani dev is solid by physical.

❖ Ghanarupa

The One with a Solid Form. Always Shani dev takes solid form in personality and decisions.

❖ - Ghanabharanadharin

The One Who Wears an Iron Ornament. Iron ore is the favorite material of Shani dev, so Shani dev always wears iron ornament.

❖ - Ghanasaravilepa

The One Anointed with Camphor. Shani dev anointed with camphor during the bath and puja. Camphor is part of a tree, and camphor makes with vapor and gas, and Shani dev indicates gases and air.

❖ - Khadyota

The Light of the Sky. Shani dev is the son of the Sun, so he is also a god of light.

❖ Manda

The Slow One. Shani dev is very slow in working.

❖ Mandacheshta

The Slow Moving One. The movement of Shani is also slow as well as Saturn also.

❖ - Mahaniyagunatman

The One with Glorious Qualities. Every pupil will be proud of god Shani.

❖ - Martyapavanapada

The one (the worship at) Whose Feet Purifies Mortals

❖ - Mahesha

The Great Lord. Here great Lord means who is always great in every stage of justice.

❖ - Chayaputra

The Son of Chaya. The mother of Shani dev is Devi Chaya (sandhya) that why calling Chayaputra.

❖ - Sharva

The One Who Injures. Shani dev can cause injuries to anyone to give punishment.

❖ Shatatuniradharin

The One Who Bears a Quiver of a Hundred Arrows. It Means Shani dev takes an arrow in the right hand to kill.

❖ Charasthirasvabhava

The One Whose Nature is to Move Steadily. Yes, it's a fact the nature of Shani dev change frequently.

❖ - Achanchala

The Steady One here the steady means Shani dev is perfect always to make decisions or state forward.

❖ Nilavarna

The Blue-Colored One. Due to complexation.

❖ - Nitya

The Eternal One. It means Shani dev is constant always by nature.

❖ - Nilanjananibha

The One with the Appearance of Blue Ointment. Shani dev wears Neelam (Blue Sapphire) on the forehead.

❖ - Nilambaravibhushana

The One Adorned with a Blue Garment. The color of the dresses of Shani dev is always blue.

❖ - Nishchala

The Steady One. Never change the decision.

❖ - Vedya

The one Who is to be known. Easy to understand, god Shani.

❖ - Vidhirupa

The one Who has the Form of the Sacred Precepts. During the Justice, Shani dev always gives a message to everyone.

❖ - Virodhadharabhumi

The Ground that Supports Obstacles. As we know, Shani dev is the god of obstacles who makes Thorn in the way of guilty.

❖ - Bhedaspadasvabhava

The One Whose Nature is the Place of Separation.

❖ Vajradeha

The one with a Body like a Thunderbolt or Levin.

❖ - Vairagyada

The Bestower of Non-Attachment. Neutral by nature.

❖ Vira

The Hero. Who has extraordinary powers?

❖ - Vitarogabhaya

The One Who is Free of Disease and Fear. There is no fear to anyone and no diseases anymore.

❖ - Vipatparamparesha

The Lord of Successive Misfortune

❖ - Vishvavandya

The One Who is Fit to be Worshipped by All. The whole universe will worship of Shani dev form may differ.

❖ - Gridhnavaha

The One Whose Mount is a Vulture. One of the Vehicles of Shani is Vulture.

❖ - Gudha

The Hidden One. Shani dev works like hiding and seek

❖ - Kurmanga

The One with the Body of a Tortoise. Clack body

❖ - Kurupin

The One with an Unusual Appearance

❖ - Kutsita

The one Who is despised

❖ Gunadhya

The One Abounding in Good Qualities

❖ - Gochara

The One Associated with the Range of the Senses (the Field of Action). Movement in the galaxy.

❖ - Avidhyamulanasha

The Destroyer of the Root of Ignorance

❖ - Vidhyaavidhyasvarupin

The One Whose Nature is Both Knowledge and Ignorance

❖ - Ayushyakarana

The Cause of Long Life. God of safe and long life.

❖ - Apaduddhartr

The Remover of Misfortune. God who can remove Misfortune

❖ - Vishnubhakta

The Devotee of Vishnu or aspect of Lord Vishnu. But Shani dev is is the advent of God Vishnu.

❖ - Vishin

The Self-Controlled One. But can not control anger.

❖ - Vividhagamavedin

The Knower of Manifold Scriptures

❖ - Vidhistutya

The One Who is Fit to be Praised with Sacred Rites

  ❖ Vandhya

The One Who is Fit to be Worshipped

  ❖ - Virupaksha

The One with Manifold Eyes

  ❖ Varishtha

The Most Excellent One in his work or his practice.

  ❖ - Garishtha

The Most Venerable One

  ❖ - Vajramkushaghara

The one who holds a Thunderbolt-Goad

  ❖ - Varadabhayahasta

The One Whose Hands Grant Boons and Remove Fear

  ❖ - Vamana

The Dwarf by personality.

  ❖ - Jyeshthapatnisameta

The One Whose Wife is Jyestha (the Devi of Misfortune, Elder Sister of Lakshmi).

  ❖ - Shreshtha

The Most Excellent One in every task, mostly injustice.

❖ - Mitabhashin

The One with Measured Speech

❖ - Kashtaughanashakartr

The Destroyer of an Abundance of Troubles

❖ - Pushtida

The Bestower of Prosperity

❖ - Stutya

The one Who is fit to Praised

❖ - Stotragamya

The One Who is Accessible through Hymns of Praise

❖ - Bhaktivashya

The one Who is subdued by Devotion

❖ - Bhanu

The Bright One. Who always shine like the Sun.

❖ Bhanuputra

The Son of Bhanu (the Sun)

❖ - Bhavya

The Auspicious One

❖ Paavana

The Purifier

❖ - Dhanurmandalasamstha

The One Who Stays in the Circle of the Bow

❖ - Dhanada

The Bestower of Wealth. Who gives you wealth like Lakshmi Mata.

❖ - Dhanushmat

The Archer. Great master in archery.

❖ - Tanuprakashadeha

The One Whose Body has a Thin Appearance

❖ - Tamasa

The One Associated with Tamoguna. It also indicates the out pathway tantra.

❖ - Asheshajanavandya

The One Who is Fit to be Worshipped by All Living Beings

❖ - Visheshaphaladayin

The Bestower of the Fruit of Discrimination

❖ - Vashikritajanesha

The Lord of Living Beings. Who has Accomplished Self-Control?

❖ - Pashunam Pati

The Lord of Animals. Every animal is a venture of Shani dev.

❖ - Khechara

The One Who Moves Through the Sky

❖ - Khagesha

The Lord of Planets

❖ Ghananilambara

The One Who Wears a Dense Blue Garment

❖ Kathinyamanasa

The Stern-Minded One. As I know, Shani dev is very strict by nature, and the mind of Shani is always stern to give punishment to the guilty.

❖ Aryaganastutya

The one Who is fit to Praised by a Multitude of Aryas. Great Arya's always praised Shani dev.

❖ - Nilachchhatra

The One with a Blue Umbrella.

❖ - Nitya

The Eternal One. Strictly follow the rules consistently.

❖ - Nirguna

The One without Attributes. No desire for self.

❖ Gunatman

The One with Attributes is the store of qualities.

❖ - Niramaya

The One Who is Free from Disease

❖ Nindya

The Blamable One

❖ Vandaniya

The One Wo is Fit to be Worshipped

❖ - Dhira

The Resolute One

❖ Divyadeha

The One with a Celestial Body

❖ - Dinartiharana

The Remover of the Suffering of Those in Distress. Remove poverty of devotees.

❖ - Dainyanashakara

The Destroyer of Affliction

❖ - Aryajanaganya

The One Who is a Member of the Arya People. Arya means who are plentiful in the community or the cast.

❖ - Krura

The Cruel One. Shani dev is cruel to criminals.

❖ - Kruracheshta

The One Who Acts Cruelly. Strict by nature and cruel for guilty.

❖ - Kamakrodhakara

The Maker of Desire and Anger. The anger of Shani dev is always on the top head.

❖ Kalatraputra-shatrutvakarana

The Cause of Hostility of Wife and Son. Who can create Misunderstanding in family

❖ - Pariposhitabhakta

The One Whose Devotees are supported. Shani dev is always safe, their devotees.

❖ - Parabhitihara

The Remover of the Greatest Fear and protect devotees.

❖ - Bhaktasanghamano-bhishtaphalada

Who gives the desired fruit to the devotees, who can read the devotee's mind to provide fruits? Now we can understand the first secret of Shani dev which is in name and also in other 108 calling names. Somewhere every name of Shani dev reflects the personality of god Shani.

The Complexion Of Lord Shani Dev

FIRST SECRET

The complexion of the Lord Shani Dev is black and blue, and I think everyone knows about this fact, but why is his complexion black? As per the Indian Mythology, Lord Surya Dev is the father of Shani, and his Mother is Chhaya. The Sun God's mother's name is Aditi, and his father's name is Maharishi Kashyap. The Sun God has two wives, namely Chhaya and Sandhya where (Chhaya is the Clone of Sandhya Devi), and Sandhya could not bear the shine of Surya Dev because his light is very high and intense. Hence, sandhya made their clone and named it Chhaya and sent it to the Surya Dev, but Chhaya is dark in her complexion, and after that, Shani dev was born with a dark face. Hence, Shani Dev is considered the son of Chhaya Devi.

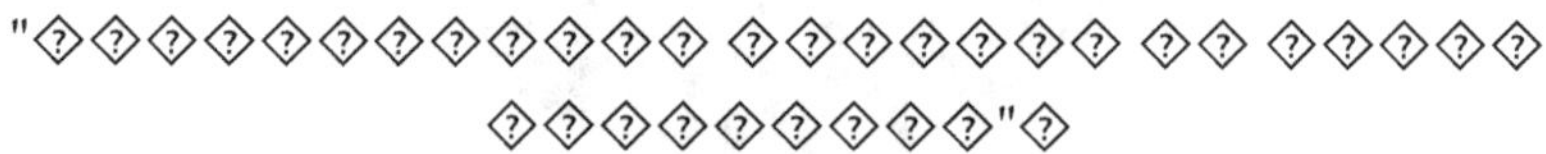

(Namskar to the son of Chhaya and Sun)

SECOND SECRET

The complexion of the Lord Shani dev and his colors of dresses are also black as I have seen that every belonging of the Lord Shani dev is related to black things. So first of all, we begin to know about the black color i.e.the black color can absorb all types of energies very fast. Also, the black color can hide anything easily under it. No color can absorb like the black one. Black color represents sadness, loneliness, punishment, etc. And the responsibility of the Lord Shani dev is making the equilibrium in nature by always punishing to the guilty natives, and here the black color itself shows that nobody can be saved to get punishment for the deed done from the path to justice by lord Shani dev. So maybe due to this reason, the lord Shani dev has adopted the black color.

Nine Vehicles Of Lord Shani Dev

To perform the karma, Shani Dev chooses his vehicle, and in the scriptures, it has been said that Lord Shani Dev has his different vehicle. Every vehicle has its importance, and every vehicle comes in action only at the desired movement of Shani dev. Crow is the essential vehicle among all the vehicles or the primary vehicle of Shani Dev. So we are going to discuss the vehicles of Shani Dev described below:

Crow

As everyone knows that the crow is black, and that's why Shani dev has chosen him as a vehicle. Secondly, the Crow is a very active bird and lightweight and can fly in the sky-high quickly. Crow is brilliant and a clever bird among all the birds. Moreover, Crow indicates the Pitru also, and pitru is very precious in Hindu mythology. The crow can adapt to every environment. Shani dev is the god of darkness, sadness, and death, and crow also indicates these types of things. The mind of a crow is very similar to that of a human mind. Crow can quickly identify the images, or we can say, can differentiate the humans in every place. Crow is a good toolmaker (creative) who can make new tools as per the availability of present things. So we can say crow is flexible enough to adapt in every situation to help Shani dev. We have already gained knowledge about the work of the Lord Shani dev as he has to move everywhere to punish the accused of guilty deeds. One fascinating thing about the crow is that it can dodge any human. Crow can neutralize the black magic things, which means any accused or guilty person can take the help of any negative energy to protect him from the Lord Shani dev, but the crow will gulp these things and neutralize the adverse effects clean the path for the Lord.

As per my knowledge, Once, Lord Shani Dev and Goddess Lakshmi were fighting as per the story of "Shree Shani Samhita." Once upon a time, Lord Shani Dev and the Goddess Laxmi (goddess of wealth) were traveling. Coincidently, they met each other on the way. After some initial conversations and exchange of whereabouts, they contradict each other by words.

Lord Shani said: - I am much better than you, as I am responsible for maintaining justice in the world.

Goddess Lakshmi replied: - That's not true, I am better than you; I give happiness, wealth, and prosperity to the world.

Lord Shani replies: - By nature itself, you are very volatile, and thus you never stay at one place for long and therefore always remain in a state of migration, also you do not discriminate between the bad and good souls....you can even stay with the evil souls.

On this Goddess, Lakshmi countered: - Stop commenting on my nature, first see yourself.

The whole world is afraid of your malefic drishti (aspect); no one wants to invite you. Everyone prays for your departure....you can only create a sense of terror.

They both decided to ask this question from "Lord Brahma (creator of the world)," So they went to Lord Brahma: - and asked the same issue.

O Lord, who is better among both of us?

Lord Brahma thought that if my answer favors Laxmi, I would not be able to escape from the malefic Drishti of Saturn. If I preferred Shani Dev, Laxmi would get angry with me, so he diplomatically said that "the answer of this question can only be given by lord Vishnu" (Sustainer of the world), So kindly, go to him." Then they moved towards The Lord Vishnu's Lok and then "Lord Vishnu" to "Lord Shiva" (the destroyer of the world) and then from Lord Shiva to "Narad muni" (Most praised devotee of Lord Vishnu and son of Lord Brahma).

Then ultimately, both of them went to "Narad Muni" and repeated the question. Who is better among both of us...? After thinking a lot, Narad Muni replied-

"Laxmi looks good when she comes, and Shani Dev looks good when he goes." In such a situation, whenever Shani Dev and Mata Lakshmi used to go from one place to another, their vehicles got used to accompanying them. In this situation, both vehicles are opposite because they wanted to see their masters as most marvelous. As we are all aware, the owl is the vehicle of Goddess Lakshmi; from that very day, both the crow and the owl attack each other as soon as they see each other. One of the best habits inside the crow is that he never flatters; he always complains about what he does not like. Crow can easily remember and recognize the human face, and in his duties towards the Lord Shani dev, it is constructive. Now I can say Shani Dev uses the crow only during excursions. And when Shani dev rides on crow, he removes his devotees' sadness and sufferings.

Vulture

Vulture is the second vehicle of lord Shani dev. But in The Indian Mythology, Vulture represents illness and non-recoverable diseases. But in actual practice, vultures can prevent diseases from spreading. The urine of vultures can kill bacterias during flying. The vulture always works to maintain the natural cycle, just like Shani Dev renews and maintains the balance of karma. A vulture has such a sharp eye that it can recognize any human from any distance. A vulture is a very courageous bird that is not ready to give up its prey under any circumstances. Just

as Shani Dev does the work of cleaning society by punishing the sinner, similarly, the vulture eats the dirt. When Shani dev uses this bird as his vehicle, we should know that the guilty will face illness and get death punishment. And when someone's punishment ends, he is free from diseases. Therefore, lord Shani dev rides on vulture to give the accused or guilty conditions.

Swan

Swan is a magnificent bird, and it indicates peace and beauty. So why did Shani dev choose this as his vehicle, whereas the area of work for Shani dev is different from the swan? Swan also symbolizes love and care as well as peace. In Hindu mythology, white swan indicates the God of Peace. Very few people know that Shani Dev is also considered a symbol of love because Shani Dev always protects true love. According to a legend, somewhere, a loving couple used to worship Shani Dev, but the villagers were against them, due to which both of them faced immense trouble. The jealous people had killed the man's wife with deception.

After that, her husband went to the shelter of Shani Dev in disconnection; Shani Dev punished everyone there and gave a chance to the man to ask for a boon. Then the dead woman's husband asks the Lord Shani dev to provide him with a promise that he will always help the true lovers. Then Shani dev replied, "Tathastu vats," and then the man asked for salvation to forget his wife's separation, and then Shani Dev converted him into a swan and took him as a vehicle. Hence, lord Shani dev rides on the swan to give peace and love in your Zodiac Sign and save your love despite whatever happens. Hans has been called the best vehicle among all Saturn vehicles.

<u>Peacock</u>

It's a well-known fact that the peacock is a dear bird to Lord Krishna. And Krishna is also the favorite God of Shani Dev, and because of this, Shani Dev keeps his favorite thing as his vehicle when Shani dev rides on peacock; it gives auspicious results to his devotees. At this time, the devotee gets good luck and hard work. The native can overcome all the great difficulties during this time if he works wisely. The economic situation can also be improved by hard work. The peacock wings are large and can fly at 65 miles per hour. In Indian mythology, peacock's wings are used to remove negative energies and other harmful things. Peacock can kill even the poison of the snake. The biggest reason for choosing a peacock is that peacock is a sign of any impending disaster. According to a story, when Shani lord was doing worship of Lord Krishna, he desired to see him. But even after many tries, he failed to see Lord Krishna, then Shani dev thinks that if he chooses the dearest thing of Lord Krishna, he may be able to see God Krishna. So Shani dev requests the peacock to stay with me during the worship of God Krishna. After this, the peacock danced with the backside of Shani dev and looked like this.

Then Lord Krishna became happy and gave him his sight. After this, Lord Krishna Said to Shani dev, "Hey, Shani, the Lord of justice, and you had used this peacock to please me, now I want to tell you you should use this peacock as your vehicle. After this incident, Shani dev uses peacock as a vehicle to go towards the justice of love and peace.

<u>**Dog**</u>

The dog is Lord Shani Dev's first and primary vehicle in a quadruped animal. Why has Shani dev chosen a dog as his primary vehicle? Many reasons are there. First of all, the dog is frank; that's why Shani dev has chosen the dog as his primary vehicle. The dog can understand the language of spirits. Dog indicates sincerity, and Shani dev likes sincerity. A dog can easily recognize the negative energy. As lord Shani dev suggests, the air and gaseous things are exciting that dogs can see the air. The dog is a clever animal and can fight with suspicious items. The smelling powers of the dogs are so sharp that Shani dev takes this vehicle to find out the guilty. But whenever Shani dev rides on a dog, the fear of theft, etc., occurs. A dog is an alert animal which is an essential thing for

the work of Shani dev.   According to a story, a devil tried to hide from Shani dev, so Shani dev had taken the dog's help and gave him an order to smell the body fragrance of everyone to find the devil as soon as possible, who was hiding on earth from him. Then the dog asked Shani dev, "Hey Lord, please ride on me, and then I will find him. Shani dev rides on the dog, and he catches the devil and then gets punished, and from that day, Shani dev rides on the dog. But there is an important thing that Shani dev always uses dark black dog.

Donkey

The donkey is a calm and straightforward animal. Once upon a time, Shani dev was going near a river where a potter was collecting mud for making pots, and he had a donkey, his name was 'Bheema.' Bheema was standing alone and waiting for his master.

When Shani Dev saw the donkey that he works hard all day long and his master does not pity him, Shani Dev thought, why not test the donkey? Shani Dev pushed his master into the water, seeing the owner falling into the water, and then the donkey started screaming. At that time, Shani dev realized that the donkey is very careful about his master, whereas his master does not care for him. That time, Lord Shani Dev thought, why not keep a donkey as a vehicle for good manners. Shani dev gave blessings to the donkey that you will always live with me as a vehicle. Now I will tell you when Shani dev rides on a donkey, and then what will happen? As I have already mentioned in the above lines, the donkey is a very calm and relaxed animal, but this animal indicates hard work and foolishness (where the mind works slowly). But when Shani dev rides on a donkey and enters in the sign of any native (who believes in astrology or whose birth chart analyzing called native). In this case, Shani dev always gives obstacles for that native. In the same manner, Shani dev always gives blocks to guilty. There is always a lack of good signs and good fruits to natives. The native will always do work hard but will get fewer results.

<u>Lion</u>

Like Lord Shani, the Lion is the Jungle-King (Forest) in Indian astrology and Kalyuga. Lion indicates a cleaver mind and good fitness. I am using the word fitness for Lion because the Lion is the fastest animal and the most potent animal that captures its prey very cleverly, and then no one can dare to snatch the game from it. Shani Dev does the same thing because no one can stop him from punishing the sinner. So somewhere, Shani Dev keeps the Lion as his vehicle and gives the message of courage and strength. As far as I know, Shani Dev is also an expert in war, and he has killed many demons. In my view, whenever Shani Dev rides on a lion, it means that Shani Dev will fight and destroy the evils. Now let's talk about the other things: when Shani Dev rides on a lion, what result does it give? First, Shani dev will provide dare, name, and fame to the native and justice. There is also a secret that Shani Dev and Rahu are good friends and Rahu rides on the Lion only after Shani Dev asks. Lion being the vehicle of Shiva, is considered auspicious. The Lion is the embodiment of victory. Therefore, the person is benefited from strong willpower, fearlessness, and power. He emerges victorious in his life at this time. The enemy's heart becomes upset whenever Shani Dev rides a lion to kill him.

Bull

Mostly, Shani dev rides on a bull, and then Shani Dev gives mixed results. Mixed results mean that they can be favorable as well as unfavorable. Therefore, one must practice caution and take decisions meticulously. Why is Shani dev using bull as a vehicle? According to my theory, once Shani dev was worshipping Lord shiva (Guru of lord Shani Dev), then Nandi (the vehicle of Shiva) felt that Shani dev was doing an excellent job for them. He is Lord Shiva's follower also, so why doesn't he join him in this great work, and then Nandi ordered the bull to live as a vehicle with Shani dev and help him always.

On the other hand, bull indicates the power and waves of anger and strength. That's why Shani dev uses the bull whenever he wants to show the accused's ability or guilt. Shani Dev does not want to live a household life but is married due to his parents. In the same way, Shani Dev analyzed that Nandi also did not accept being a householder and is constantly ready to serve his Guru? It is also a reason to adopt bull as a vehicle. When Shani dev rides on a bull, then he takes a sword in his hand to kill the enemies. When Shani dev walks with the bull in the sky, they can reach in any lok to search the guilty. One fantastic thing is that whenever Shani dev visits any lok to explore the guilty encountering barriers on his way, the bull can crack all the obstacles with his horn.

Elephant

Elephants are essential in Indian mythology too. Lord Ganesha, one of the most popular Indian deities and the Lord of Wisdom, bears an elephant head. The elephant head symbolizes excellent intellect and wisdom. Elephants symbolize royalty - Maharajas and kings used to ride during processions and wars on elephants. When Shani Dev was declared the King of the Shani Lok, Shani Dev accepted the elephant as a vehicle, then Shani Dev is also known as Shani Maharaj.

One of the biggest things is that whenever Shani Dev comes on an elephant, he gives wealth; this vehicle belongs to Lord Ganesha. According to a legend, Shani Dev is always normal and decent, and he does not like showing off. Once Goddess Lakshmi asked him in arrogance, "Lord Ganesha,

and all other Devgans, have an elephant as a royal ride." But as a king of Shani Loka, you do not have any royal ride." and then Shani dev adopted the elephant as his royal ride.

Lord Shani Dev Is The Lord Of Kalyuga

Nowadays, the prevailing Yuga is the Yuga of kali, i.e., Kaliyuga. The era in which we live is known as Kalyuga, and the Lord of this era is Lord Shani Dev. Now let's discuss why it is so? According to Indian mythology, few reasons are given to understand why Shani is the dev of Kalyuga? As per the deeds of every person, Kalyuga is full of sins and crime, so as discussed earlier, the workload of Lord Shani has been increased. People are more dependent on modern scientific articles and machines these days. We can say that people have become more materialistic in this Yuga; hence the term Kalyuga (Kal meaning component) is appropriate. And secondly, it could also be linked with the color & complexion of Lord Shani dev that indicates the black color, and so the color of Kalyuga is also black.

> **Reason-1** In Vedic astrology, outer space, wastelands, cemeteries, forests and deep deserts, deep valleys, mountains, caves, trenches, mines, and all resident free places on this earth, falls under the jurisdiction of Saturn. Thus, Shani Dev's jurisdiction includes deep and secret knowledge and all our vigilance-related tasks like labor, service, helplessness, hindering persons, and helping ill and older people. During the unfavorable period of Saturn, one has to face endless sorrow; Opportunities also exist for loss of wealth and health. One can easily be humiliated if indulged in wrong deeds or even get incurable diseases. And all these things are present mainly in Kaliyuga only; hence it can be believed that this era belongs to Shani Dev.

> **Reason-2** According to a Pauranik Katha (Legend Story), there was some time left in the completion of the Pandavas' thirteen years of exile. The five Pandavas and Draupadi were looking for a place to splash in the forest, while Shani Dev's eyes were fallen on the Pandavas from the sky. Then sudden

thought strikes his mind who is wise among all of these, and test should be. Shani Dev built a Maya's Palace in many paths. The four corners of that palace were east, west, north, and south. Suddenly, Bhima's eyes fell on the palace, attracting him. Bhima said to Yudhishthira - Brother, I want to see the castle. When Bhima reached the palace gate, Shanidev stood as a concierge; his elder brother agreed. Bhima asked him to visit the palace, Shani Dev replied that.

"There are some rules of this palace, you can see only one corner from the four corners of the palace, and then you will have to explain the essence of what you will see in the castle. If you are not able to explain, you will be imprisoned. Bhima accepted the rules and went towards the east end of the palace. Going there, he looked at the beautiful animals and birds and trees laden with flowers and fruits; going ahead, he came to see that there are three wells, small in the vicinity and a big well in the middle. The large middle well was filled with water and filled both the small wells with water the rules, and he went towards the east end of the palace. Going there, he looked at the beautiful animals and birds and trees laden with flowers and fruits; going ahead, he came to see that there are three wells, small in the vicinity and a big well in the middle. The large middle well was filled with water and filled both the small wells. Then after some time, there was a boom in both the small wells, but only half the water of the big well remained. Bhima has seen this action many times but cannot understand it and returns to the concierge. Concierge - What did you see? Bhima - Sir, I have seen such plants, animals, and birds that I have never seen before. I did not understand why small wells were filled with water; I did not understand why they could not fill it.

The concierge said, " You are captive as per the condition " Bhima was put in the prison house.

Arjuna came and asked - I want to see the palace; then, the concierge described the rules, and Arjuna went towards the western end. Going forward, Arjuna has seen that two crops were growing in one field, millet on one side and maize crop on the other side. Maize was coming out from the millet plant and millet from the maize plant. I did not understand anything; he came back to the entrance door. The concierge asked what he saw. Arjuna replied that he saw everything but did not understand the issue of millet and maize. Shani Dev said, according to the rule, you are captive. Nakula came and asked, I have to see the palace; then he went towards the north, where he saw that many white cows drink the milk of their little heifer when they felt hungry. Nakula did not understand anything. The concierge asked what he saw? Nakula answered that he did not know that the cow drinks the heifer's milk; why so? Later, Sahadev asked to see the palace, and he went towards the south to see the last corner. He saw a big stone of gold that does not fall on the staggered dole, which rests on a silver coin, remains the same on touching it. He did not understand that, and he came back to the door and said that he could not understand the matter of the golden stone, and then he too was imprisoned.

When the four brothers did not come back from the palace, Yudhishthira was worried that he also went with Draupadi. The concierge said he was imprisoned as per the rules when asked for the brothers.

Yudhishthira asked, what did you see, Bhima? Bhima told about the well. Then Yudhishthira said - this will happen in Kali Yuga, one father will fill the stomach of two sons, but two sons together will not be able to fill the stomach of one father. Bhima was released. What did you see, Arjun? He told about the crop, Yudhishthira said- It is also going to happen in the Kali Yuga, i.e., the change of dynasty, i.e., the girl of the house of Brahman and the girl of Shudra will be married in the home of the bride. Arjuna was also released. What did you see, Nakula? Then he told the incident of the cow, then Yudhishthira said - In Kali Yuga, mothers will grow up in their daughters' house, eat daughter's grain and sons will not serve her. Then Nakula too was released. What did you see, Sahadeva? Yudhishthira asked; he answered about the account of the rock of gold, then Yudhishthira said - Sins will continue to suppress religion in Kali Yuga, but the faith will remain alive.

All the four brothers were released. Shanidev believed that Yudhishthira was the most intelligent. According to the story, everything is, and I will be called Dev of Kalyuga (kali happening in Kali Yuga). Then Shani Dev says that the era in which all this will happen is the Kaliyuga). Shani Dev was the first god to show the Kali Yuga to the Pandavas. After all, all these did not occur in Treta Yuga, and all this is possible only in Kali Yuga. Perhaps the Leela that Shani Dev had created was the beginning of the Kali-yuga. For this reason, also, Shani Dev is called the God of Kali-yuga.

> **Reason-3** Shani Dev is the Unforgiving Lord, and due to this, it can be said that Shani dev is the Lord of Kalyuga. Shani Dev is considered a very strict deity due to his brutal nature and discipline. Until Shani dev does not punish the guilty person, he can not forgive anyone. Shani Dev does this to show the right path to the sinner by punishing him for his karma. If someone regrets his evil deeds, then Shani Dev forgives him with significantly less punishment, and if not, he will surely punish him. Shani dev will do this when his Justice chakra comes in a cycle for the sinners. I will discuss one story that shows the unforgiving nature of Shani dev. It is essential to understand about Shani Dev that he is furious and stubborn, and once he gets irritated by someone, he does not let him live. Or if anyone tries to show him an ego, then Shani Dev takes every possible way to break his ego.

Lord Shani Dev Was Born From Fire

46

AS WE ALL KNOW, LORD Shani Dev's father is the Sun God, and the Sun God represents the Agni. That is why Shani Dev is said to have been born out of Agni. Moreover, Shani Dev was born from the fire, clearly shown in his eyes, representing fire flames. The anger of Shani Dev is so piercing that it shows fire flames in his gestures. When Lord Shani was in his mother's womb, he was total; being in the womb turned black. Therefore, Lord Shani was utterly black in his complexion at his birth. Also, Lord Shani Dev had to suffer the outbreak of his father, which is like a fierce fire. Agni Putra Shani Dev is not called by this name only because he punished his father when the Sun God thought he was beautiful and how his son could be black? And due to which the Sun God doubted Chhaya, and for that reason, Lord Shani Dev got angry with his father and punished him.

Lord Shani Is An Unforgiving God

$\mathbf{S}$ hani Dev is counted among the strict deities due to his uncompromising nature and disciplinary behavior. Until the Lord does not punish the guilty, he cannot forgive anyone. Shani Dev does this to show the right path to the sinner by punishing him for his karmas. If someone regrets his evil deeds, then the Lord forgives him by giving him less punishment, and if not, he will surely punish that sinner, and Lord Shani dev will do this when his justice chakra comes in a cycle on the sinners. I am presenting a short story that will show the unforgiving nature of the Lord Shani dev, and it is essential to understand that Lord Shani Dev is very angry and stubborn, and that's why, once he gets irritated by someone, he does not let him live. Or if anyone tries to show him an ego, then Shani Dev can take any route to break his ego.

Shani Dev and King Vikramaditya

Once upon a time in the kingdom of Malwa (Now presently called Indore and Ujjain areas). In the capital city of Ujjain, there was a king named Vikramaditya. Vikram was a righteous and heroic king; he had been loved and respected by all the citizens of his state. Once in the court of the King, he asked a question to the pandits. Which planet is best in Navgrah, then every Pandit explained the quality of their planet.

First, Pandit replied, "The greatest of all the planetary Lords is the Sun, Lord Suryanarayan or the Sun God. You can be able to see him every day in the sky as every day begins with him. He bestows good health to the entire planet, and the only Sun is the dev seen in the Kalyuga.

The second Pandit answered: The scriptures say the Lord of the Moon is Lord Soma. He is a gardener by his caste. Moon is the one who looks after the vegetation on this planet. Being calm in temperament, he does not bother anyone. An eternal servant of Lord Mahadev, he permanently resides on his head and hence is the greatest".

Third Pandit, "that Mangal Devata is a goldsmith from caste and is the most powerful planet, he is a cruel planet, and if we pray to Mangal Dev, he gives everything but Rajan, be careful, "an egoic prayer gets punishment."

The fourth one says, "It is Lord Budha, the Lord of the planet Mercury who is the greatest of all of them. He is a trader by caste and bestows wealth when he gets pleased. He is good and does not harass anyone. Hence, O' King now considers him to be the greatest.

Fifth Pandit Says, "Lord Brihaspati, the master of the planet Jupiter is the greatest of all the planets. Out of the four castes, Lord Brihaspati is a Brahmin. Therefore, consider him to be the greatest. He is the spiritual preceptor of the Gods and is not angered by anyone. He is at peace with all as a true realized soul and wishes the best for everyone".

Sixth, Pandit Says, "Lord Bhargava, the ruler of the planet Venus, is the preceptor of the demons. He created the Sanjivani Mantra, a mystical chant that would bring the dead to life. Highly regarded among the Gods and Demons, consider him the greatest", as said the sixth Pandit.

Seventh Pandit Says, "Rahu and Ketu are two of the cruelest planets. They do not show mercy to anyone. But they show some leniencies to those who pray to them and offer sacrifices to them. Rahu plagues the Moon, and Ketu troubles the Sun. One can see the Eclipses as a sign of this"

Next, Pandit Says, "Shani is the most fantastic planet among the nine planets. He is furious by nature and an unforgiving planet. When he is pleased, Shani can bestow all that is good, and when someone angers him, it can be the reason for complete ruin. He causes anxiety and vexes the mind. He causes bodily suffering, but he bestows the glory that lasts an eternity.

When the King listened to this, King Vikramaditya laughed and said, "Of what use is a son whose birth brings about suffering for his father. Such a person is an enemy and not a son" King said this; then all the members began to laugh. When Shani dev listened to this insult, he came to the court on his vehicle crow and said, "Rajan, you have made fun of me, I will come in your zodiac sign and punish only through the Kanya (Girl). As soon as Lord Shani entered his zodiac to punish the King, the King started worshiping Lord Shiva to avoid the punishment of Lord Shani Dev, but Lord Shiva could not save him, and Shani Dev punished him. Finally, the King had apologized to Shani Dev and said that my entire ego had been destroyed. So as per this story, we can say that Shani dev is the unforgiving god, and it is pretty easy to make him angry, but it is not easy to make him calm down. Shani dev is also the god of death, who can give a punishment equal to the end of life.

Why Is Mustard Oil Offered To Lord Shani Dev?

You must have seen that mustard oil is offered to Shani Dev to worship him; however, it has become a trend nowadays. Many of us are still unaware of this. Knowing when and who can offer oil to Shani Dev is necessary. According to a story, we can understand why we offer Shani dev.

First Legend

In childhood, Shani dev was very naughty, bothering everyone. According to the legend, when Lord Rama's army tied the Sagar Setu, the demons could not harm it, for that Pawansut Hanuman was entrusted with the care of the Setu. Lord Hanuman was active meditation with his presiding deity Rama; Lord Shani made his ugly black face. He retorted, O monkey, I am the powerful God Shani among all the gods. I have heard you are very powerful, Open your eyes and fight with me; I want to fight with you. In this message, Lord Hanuman politely said that - At this time, I am remembering my Lord. Do not disturb my attention. You are my honor; please go from here.

Shani Dev felt that no one should be stronger than him, but this was his childish thought. When Shani Dev reached down to fight, Lord Hanuman wrapped him in his big tail. Then he began to tighten him, applying stress, and Saturn did not get rid of that bondage and started getting distraught with pain. Lord Hanuman revolves around the bridge and starts banging his tail on the stones to break Shani's arrogance. It caused Shani's body to bleed, which increased his suffering. Then Shani Dev prayed to Lord Hanuman to make him free and said," you have taught me a lesson for my false ego, and now I will not make such a mistake! Again". Then Lord Hanuman gave mustard oil to Shani dev and asked him to apply this oil on the wound to get rid of the pain. Oil is offered to Shani dev from the same day, which calms his suffering, and he becomes happy. Due to the grace of Lord Hanuman, the suffering of Lord Shani Dev was down, and that is why even today, Shani maintains special blessings on the devotees of Lord Hanuman.

Second Legend

In his childhood, Shani dev was very angry and always used to fight with other Children. It was his habit to get hyper on every matter. We can say that Shani dev cannot live with anyone or adjust. Once upon a time, he got angry with his parents for something, and they left the house. After that, his mother continued to be troubled and restless. She went to Surya Dev, but the father did not answer anything in displeasure and said," Devi! You can ask for help from Lord Hanuman".

Then Mother of Shani dev requested Lord Hanuman and shared everything about Shani dev's anger. Then Lord Hanuman gets ready to find out Shani dev to hand him over to his mother.

Lord Hanuman then began to find out Shani dev, but as Shani dev is also illusive who can make illusions to anyone. Shani Dev got to know that his parents had sent Lord Hanuman to find him, and he would not come into the hands of Hanuman because he was thought to be very powerful compared to Lord Hanuman. But the interesting fact is that the Guru of Lord Hanuman is Surya dev and Shani dev is the son of Surya dev, and this fight got so complicated as at the one side, and he was to find the Sun of his Guru (Surya dev). On the other hand, there was the responsibility of his Guru dharma.

Shani dev often made an illusion to hide his body from Lord Hanuman. Shani Dev made a black mountain and hides in it. And when sunlight falls on that mountain and the mountain absorbs the energy of the Sun, and when Lord Hanuman looks at the hill, it will look different. So Lord Hanuman struck on the mountain, and he realized that it was not an ordinary mountain and he threw the mountain in the river and then Shani dev came out of the mountain and hid immediately.

The next day, Shani dev got furious and destroyed many things of nature. Everywhere, there was an atmosphere of fear. The whole Devlok was scared and was thinking about the next move of Shani dev. Lord Hanuman got to know about the same by someone when Lord Shani Dev was destroying the natural things and giving trouble to others living beings. The Lord went there and said to Shani dev, "Hey, Shani Dev, come with me and stop doing this action as soon as possible.

Shani Dev said to Lord Hanuman, "You cannot catch me. I am the most powerful god". When Lord Shani was going to hide from lord hanuman, then lord Hanuman requested him again, "Hey, Shani dev, your mother is getting worried about you, you should go back to your home. But Shani dev did not agree with Lord Hanuman, and then the Lord lifted his Gada and called upon Shani Dev for a fight. Hanuman Ji fought with Shani dev with his powers. When Shani dev began to feel weak, he tried to hide inside a house, but Lord Hanuman found him and began to fight again. Now, lord Shani struck on lord hanuman and started fighting with him. Lord Hanuman again lifted his Gada and attacked Shani dev.

Both Deities had stronger powers, and nature had also been affected by their battle. Lord Shani Dev was failing in the war. Shani dev tried to push a snake towards The Lord Hanuman at that time. And the Lord then killed the snake with an arrow, and then the Lord absorbed all the weapons of Shani dev under his control. In the battle, Shani dev was injured and was bleeding from everywhere, and then he finally surrendered to Lord Hanuman and apologized before him for fighting with him. After that, the Lord lifted Shani dev and went towards the Surya Lok (his home). When he reached there, the mother of Shani dev was happy to see him at her first glance, but as she saw the condition of Shani dev, she got scared and began to cry and plead before the Lord, "Hey Hanuman! Please save my son and give him some treatment so that he can get well soon". Then the Lord offered mustard oil to Shani Dev's mother and said, "Hey Mata apply this oil on the wound of Shani dev, and he will get well soon," and Shani dev was well after a few days. Afterward, Shani dev called upon Lord Hanuman and proposed him for friendship. From that very day, Lord Shani Dev and Lord Hanuman became good friends, and after this incident, everyone offered mustard oil to Shani dev to calm him.

Shiva Is The Guru Of Lord Shani Dev

NO ONE CAN FIND A WAY of life without a Guru because the Guru will destroy your evil deeds and show you the right path of karma. Unless you don't see the right Guru, you can not understand the logic of your life. As mentioned above, Lord Shani Dev was an angry child. As he was fast and powerful, i.e., enough to be the son of the Sun, it was his nature to know everything immediately and preserve the knowledge gained. It was his very nature to fight with his siblings all the time and to grieve everyone in stubbornness. When The Sun God comes to know about the condition of Shani Dev, he feels terrible. He decided to give some responsibility to the Lord but could not provide any responsibility for him. The Sun God was unable to assign any commitment to his son Shani. Then, the Sun God requested Lord Vishnu about Shani dev destiny.

And after listening to this matter, Lord Vishnu answered to Lord Sun, "Hey Surya Dev, I completely understand the whole situation of yours and Shani." Still, I want to tell you the truth about Shani dev that Shani dev is my advent, who will take a significant responsibility, and the conversation began as below:

Lord Vishnu: Hey, Surya dev, I told you about Shani dev.

Surya Dev: "Pranam Dev! What is the following order for Shani or me?

Lord Vishnu: Hey Surya Dev, I can give any responsibility to Shani because he is my advent. So it's my order to you, you should go to Lord Shiva for knowing the true destiny of Shani.

Surya Dev: Please, bless my son and permit me to go there.

Lord Vishnu replied with, "Tathasthu."

Surya dev gets happy after listening to this, and he went to the Suryalok, and lord Shani dev was summoned by him then, and a conversation began:

Surya Dev: "Hey, Son Shani, Come With me; we will go to The Kailash Parvata and meet Lord Shiva."

Shani: As you say, PitahShree.

When Lord Suryanarayan and Shani Dev reached over the Kailash Parvata, they saw Lord Shiva in Samadhi. And when Shiva came out of his Samadhi and greeted Surya Dev, "welcome Dev."

LORD SHIVA: I know why you both have come here, Surya Dev. You are worried about your son Shani Dev.

Surya Dev: Yes, Lord, you are an intermediary.

Lord Shiva: As you know that, "Shani is the advent of Lord Vishnu."

Surya Dev: Hey," Adidev Bhagwan Shiv! Please give some direction to my son Shani".

Then Lord Shiva: "Hey Shani, now the time has come for you to know about yourself and your work (Responsibility)."

Shiva: Shani dev, I will give you a very responsible work, that nobody can do that work except you.

Surya Dev: Hey Lord, will Shani be able to do this type of work?

Lord Shiva- Hey, Surya Dev, Shani was born from fire, and he is your son, and so that, Shani has extraordinary powers, that's why I think only Shani dev can do this work.

Surya Dev: But my Lord, what type of work will you give to Shani?

Lord Shiva: I am giving responsibility to Shani to do justice.

And the Lord Shani dev agreed with this responsibility, but Surya Dev was shocked to listen to this.

Surya Dev Says: Hey Adidev Shiv! My Lord, You have created this world, you have made everything, and you know everything. But with apologies, I want to ask something.

Lord Shiva: Hey Surya Dev, ask me, please.

Surya Dev: Hey Adidev Bhagwan Shiva, nobody can understand their responsibility, and Shani has no guru so far.

Then Lord Shiva replied, "Yes, you are right, Surya dev. Lord Shiva was thinking upon the same, and then suddenly, Shani Dev said, "Hey Adidev Bhagwan Shiv, you are giving me a significant responsibility, and whenever I will need help regarding that, I will remember you or ask from you. And that's why I want to make you my Guru, and by this, my problems will get solved.

Lord Shiva: Ok, Shani, from today onwards, I am your Guru, now perform your Guru Pujan, and then adopt you as my Shishya.

Shani Dev did the Guru Pujan and took Deeksha from Lord Shiva and blessed him by Lord Shiva. From that day, Lord Shiva becomes the Guru of Shani dev.

And Lord Shiva had given the primary responsibility to Lord Shani Dev. He advised him, "O Shani Dev! you are the deity now because you are going to do justice to everyone, no matter whom." Shani dev will need more powers to destroy the sins for this work. Then Lord Shiva ordered Goddess Mahakali, "O Goddess Kali (Parvati), I have now completed my work, and now you will give the powers to Shani Dev" so he will become powerful. Give him The Tantra Shakti and the ability to fly, give him the power to disguise, and then Surya dev and Shani dev took the permission from Lord Shiva to go for the work.

Secrets In The Four Arms Of Lord Shani Dev

SHANI DEV HAS FOUR arms and in his four arms, there rests different positions and weapons. Every component is for a unique task as well as a weapon. However, the eyes of Shani dev are used to find the sinners. At the same time, the four arms of Shani dev are used to kill sins. Now I am going to discuss the arms quality of Shani dev. In the arm of Shani dev, it has weapons that I will examine.

First Armor Weapon of Shani Dev (Right Side Beside)

Trishul/Trident- - It is the first weapon of Shani dev called Trishul (Means Three Sharp forks in the same direction, the middle fork (prong) is large compared to another two). This weapon is also used by the Guru of Lord Shani Dev, i.e., Lord Shiva. The trident is meant to destroy evil to maintain peace in the world and maintain Dharma.

The first weapon of Shani dev indicates the defender. Trishul as weapon provided by the Shiva to Shani dev. In Indian mythology, Trishul symbolizes the power of the trident. The first fork symbolizes Lord Bharmha, the Middle Fork symbolizes Lord Shiva, and the third fork symbolizes Lord Vishnu. The unit power of the trident makes Trishul. The Trishul in the human body represents the three energy channels, i.e., Ida, Pingala, and Sushumna, meeting at the brow. Trishul of Lord Shiva has Damroo, but in the Trishul of Shani dev, it is not Damroo. Trishul can destroy the sin and the sinners because Trishul represents the trinity. Brahma, Vishnu, and Mahesha are the principal gods of this universe, so the trinity's power is more than others.

Shani dev will use this weapon to kill the sinner. He can use this weapon to kill anyone (Primarily the Criminals). This weapon is used only to destroy sin and not for mercy and not for defense; it is used only to end anyone. Shani dev keeps this weapon in his first right hand.

Alternative Weapon Sword

Most of the time, Shani dev uses Sword to kill the sinners. The Goddess Mahakali gives this weapon at the time of power distribution by Mahakali. This weapon shows the edge and sharpness of Goddess Mahakali. This weapon only has one part, and it is beneficial to kill or destroy anybody. In the battle with the devil, Shani dev uses this weapon, mainly used with a bull vehicle.

Second Arm (Left Side Above)

On the other hand, Shani dev has a bow.

Bow and Arrow- Second weapon Lord Shani Dev uses as a long-distance attacker. At the same time, the bow is an ideal weapon in Devtas (among all the gods). Even Lord Shiva also uses this weapon to kill Sinners. The bow is a weapon that can strike with lots of power through arrows. The arrows that Shani Dev use are mighty and also miraculous. There was a battle between King Dasharat and Shani Dev when Shani Dev defeated King Dasharat with a bow and arrow. So we can simply conclude that the bow-arrow is a powerful weapon of Shani dev. Shani dev uses this weapon only to defeat the accused and not destroy. This weapon was also given to Shani Dev by Lord Shiva.

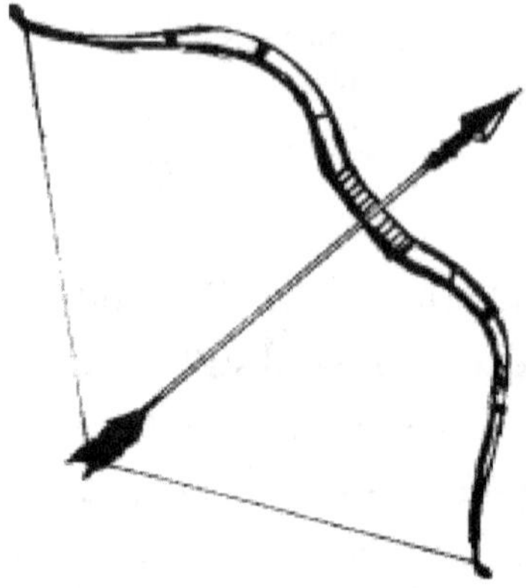

This weapon is also used for defending many weapons. Shani dev keeps this weapon in his first left hand. This weapon has three essential parts, i.e., the first one is a thread, the second one is the arrow, and the third is Limb. Where the rope represents the Bharma and Limb shows Lord Vishnu, and the arrow shows the power of Lord Shiva. Shani dev keeps this weapon with any of his vehicles. The arrow, which shows the power of lord shiva, can defeat, defend, and kill anyone, but this arrow is mainly used for beating.

Third Arm (Left Side Lower Arm) Bludgeon (Gada): Gada is the third weapon of lord Shani dev used during the mini battles. Lord Vishnu gave this weapon to Lord Shani dev. Bludgeon shows the extreme source of power. Shani Dev has used mace (Bludgeon) only to bring the sinner on the right path through it has never killed anyone.

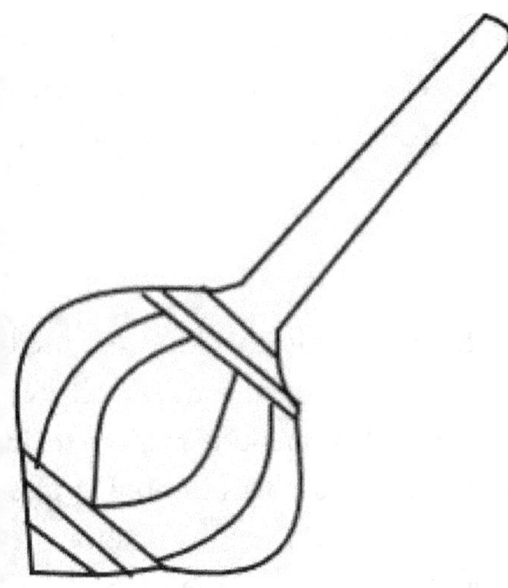

Shani Dev's mace works like medicine, suppressing the enemy with its power. The central part of the mace is the dome; energy is collected and transferred to the one who falls. Just as the mother earth revolves around the Sun God and collects & stores vitality from it, in the same way, mace rounds the body to manage the energy used by its physician, symbolizing immense physical strength, masculinity, and glory.

There is an interesting fact about this weapon that Lord Vishnu used for the first time. However, there is one story behind this. Gada was the name of a mighty Asura (demon) who once brought an abundance of terror upon humanity, but he was also quite charitable. Many legends have told about how terrible Gada was, but he had one flaw that was relatively easy to take advantage of or can say one of his weaker points. Gada never refused a request. Whatever was asked of him, no matter how ridiculous the request might be, he would be ready to do that. Lord Vishnu decided to resolve the worse situation, and in doing so, he became the creator of the Gada Mace. Lord Vishnu disguised himself as a Brahmin poet and approached Gada, requesting to lend him his bones. Happy to serve, Gada ripped himself apart at the seams to deliver his bones to Lord Vishnu. Lord Vishnu then took those bones and fashioned himself as the grandest Gada Mace of all time. So as I have discussed earlier in the above lines, Shani dev is the incarnation of Lord Vishnu, which could be one of the reasons for this weapon to be carried by Shani Dev. Shani dev keeps mace in his left hand, and Lord Vishnu holds the same in his left hand too.

Var Mudra (Right Side Lower Arm)

This Mudra is also known as Hitkari Mudra. Mainly, this Mudra is used to give blessings to the pupils. When somebody comes to the shelter of Lord Shani dev, he gives him his benefits. If somebody realizes their karma and wants to apologize, Shani Dev will bless that person. Despite being strict by his behavior, who never forgives one easily, if someone comes to realize his bad karma, he will indeed be forgiven by him. Because of this, Shani dev is considered a soft-hearted god in Indian mythology who always respects the actual phases of life and love, faith, and responsibility.

He only gives darshan to his devotees in this Mudra; otherwise, not all. This Mudra is only for the welfare, and no one gets hurt. This posture also shows how generous he is, and the great Shani Dev falls under the category of cruel and gives welfare to his devotees. His brutal nature was not only to punish the accused.

Worship Of Shani In Night

Shani dev is the god of the night because he is the god of darkness. If we see the Saturn planet, we find that Saturn is made of dust and small stones continuously revolving in the air. But if we talk about the Shani dev, then Shani is also the god of darkness and sadness. Sun is the father of Shani dev, and Sun is the god of light and shine. But at the time of birth of Shani, his color was very dark and his eyes.

When Surya Dev saw the Shani dev for the first time, he was shocked and angry. He was reflecting the fire. Because Surya is very shiny and fair by complexion, his son is just the opposite.

So Surya dev was angry, but when Shani dev listened to these words from his mother. Then he decides to punish the Surya dev. Then Shani dev declares that my father, Surya dev, thinks I am not like him. So now it will always be done if my

Father is east; then I am west; if my father is light, I am dark. If the timing of worship of my father is in daylight, then my worship will do after the sunset. After this incident, Shani dev neutralizes the power of Surya dev. Then Surya Dev realizes that nobody can balance my energy except me; Shani is mine. From that day, the worship of Shani dev will come after the sunset. We should do worship Shani dev only after the sunset. Many reasons are there; the first one is Shani dev comes on earth after the 1st part of the night (9.00 pm), so this time is good for worship and Tantrik puja of Shani dev. The second Reason is Shani dev lives in the west direction and this direction of darkness & night. Shani Dev is a God who is calm by nature, who does not like an excessive stall, and all this can be possible even at night. Hence the worship time of Shani Dev can also be considered as night. One thing also comes to my mind that nighttime is for sinners like theft etc. Shani Dev can quickly identify the sinners by riding on his vehicle.

You Can Not Make Lockup To Lord Shani

es, it is all true that nobody can capture the Lord Shani dev as the Lord is always considered the God of Freedom. He is the one who is capable of visiting any Loka being (MrityuLok, Devlok, and SwargLok). According to the legend, King Ravana of Lanka, an ascetic, Mahayodha, is elusive. He was also an ardent devotee of Lord Shiva. Once he did austerities and received a boon from Brahma Ji that the hands of anyone would not kill him but only humans and apes, and after getting a boon, he became egoistic and began to hang Lord Shani dev and Kaal (the time). Then both of them began to remember their Lord Shiva by crying and praying to him, and then Lord Shiva appeared after hearing the pain of his devotees and assured both that he would come soon to save them in the form of Lord Hanuman. When the tyranny of Ravana started increasing, Lord Vishnu was incarnated as Rama and the Goddess Lakshmi as Prithviputri Sita to kill him. Later, when Rama took exile to obey his father's order, Prithviputri Sita and his anuj Laxmana started living in the forest.

Chinkas like Ravana's Khar, Sorrow, and Trishira were killed in the war. In retaliation, Ravana kidnaps Goddess Sita by deceit and hides in his Ashoka Vatika in Lanka. One day Ravana's sister Shurpanakha went there to spread her Maya and insisted Rama-Laxman for a war. Lords Rama-Lakshmana met Rudravatar Hanuman simultaneously, and then the search for Sita began.

Lord Hanuman crossed Lanka to search for Sita and entered Lanka and met the Goddess Sita, who was imprisoned in the Ashoka Vatika of Ravana. After meeting Devi Sita, Lord Hanuman started eating Ashoka Vatika's fruits and caused destruction. Then, Ravana sent his son Akshay Kumar to stop him, but Lord Hanuman killed Akshay Kumar. In the end, Meghnath imprisoned Lord Hanuman and presented him in front of Ravana by holding him in the Brahmapash, and Ravana decided to set fire to Lord Hanuman's tail. The Lord demolished Lanka with his burning tail, but he did not see the Shyam Varna (black color) even when the whole city of Lanka was burning. Then his eyes fell on Lord Shani Dev in the imprisonment of Ravana. Then Shani dev narrated his agony to Lord Hanuman that Ravana has also taken his powers. Then Lord Hanuman Freed Shani Dev. Then Lanka burned into ashes. After this, Ravana had destroyed, and his dynasty was in the Rama-Ravana war. Later the Lord Hanuman freed the Kaal also.

Then Shani dev said to Lord Hanuman that, "O Mahavir! I will continue to be your companion. Then Lord Hanuman performed his Rudra form while offering Shani Dev divine power. At that time, Lord Shani dev took hold of Lord Hanuman's feet and started shedding tears of love. He told Hanuman, "Lord, I will never torment your devotees." I will protect the person who will read or listen to this story; I will protect him always. So by using this story, I am trying to say that if an influential person like

Ravana failed to capture Lord Shani Dev then. Who would be able to do it?

That's why the temple of Shani dev should not be locked or could not use any locking system. As in the actual practice in Signapur village, there is no locking system in houses and temples. So it can be said there is no lock in the temple of Lord Shani Dev.

In Indian Tantra, one remedy is prevalent to remove the harmful effects of the Lord Shani dev. If somebody puts a few almonds inside the black cloth and fixes it at a black storeroom by diffusing the mantra of Shani dev, then day by day, he will be rich and healthy. But by mistake, if the sunlight falls on this Pothri containing the black cloth and almonds, then on that day, the native will lose everything; it's a practical experiment in The Indian Tantra.

One more Yantra Experiment in India Tantra is the one yantra that if you throw the yantra "Shani Dosha Nivaran Yantra" in the well by writing it on the bhojpatra, then Lord Shani Dev will remove all the harmful effects soon. Still, if by chance the person drinks the water of that well, then the person will quickly begin to lose everything, and also, even if the person visits that well again in his whole life, that person will lose everything soon.

www.ingramcontent.com/pod-product-compliance
Lightning Source LLC
Chambersburg PA
CBHW061257140726
47998CB00006B/2247